Michael Bland has driven everything from a bubble car to a tank (and still has difficulty remembering which is which). He currently clocks up over 20,000 miles a year driving to and from his job as a public relations manager with a top motor manufacturer, which allows him unlimited opportunities to observe – with untiring fascination and perpetual disbelief – the antics of his fellow road-users.

He is the author of three textbooks on communications and has also written several items for TV and radio comedy shows – mostly dreamed up while dodging the wheels of 30-ton juggernauts and 90-mph company reps on the A12 near his home in Colchester.

Derek Chambers now takes the train from his home in Hockley, Essex, to work in London, where he is a partner in a design consultancy firm. He has decided that driving does not suit his profession – the drawing board kept getting in the way of the steering wheel. His previous activities, which allowed plenty of scope for driving, included travelling round the world as a photographer on assignment for *Newsweek* magazine. He is married with a daughter and two sons, all of whom are hell-bent on beating their father's impressive record for collecting parking fines.

A Pig at the Wheel

Michael Bland

Illustrations by Derek Chambers

Hamlyn Paperbacks

A Hamlyn Paperback

Published by Arrow Books Limited

17-21 Conway Street, London W1P 6JD

A division of the Hutchinson Publishing Group

London Melbourne Sydney Auckland
Johannesburg and agencies throughout
the world

First published in Great Britain 1983
by Hamlyn Paperbacks
Reprinted 1983

Text © 1983 by Michael Bland
Illustrations © 1983 by Derek Chambers

Printed and bound in Great Britain by
Anchor Brendon Limited, Tiptree, Essex

ISBN 0 600 20801 X

CONTENTS

INTRODUCTION

First, the good news. There are 208,453 miles of road in Britain. These have been laid exclusively for *your* personal use to give *you* the freedom to get into your car and travel where you will, when you will.

Now the bad news. There are also 23,599,999 other drivers, all of whom seem to think that the roads have been laid for *their* convenience, not yours. Worse still, there are nearly two million lorries, who neither know nor care whose road it is.

People talk about the personal freedom and mobility of the car but the plain truth is that nothing outside Parkhurst prison is less free. Before you even get into your car you are tied up in regulations and taxes, and if ever you have the perseverance to actually get the thing on to the road it's a miracle if you can get more than ten yards without falling foul of some rule or other. Dammit, there's even a white line down the middle of the road which only lets you use half the road at a time!

And it's getting worse. Not only are there more regulations; not only is the cost of motoring shooting up like a rat up a drainpipe, but every year there are more and more cars and lorries *and* more and more drivers. And these vehicles are not spread evenly over the surface of the country. Most of them tend to congregate along the one stretch of road on which you happen to be driving.

Thus today's motorist needs ever higher standards of pig-headedness, mindless determination and total lack of consideration for others. You *must* remember that only *you* know the first thing about driving. Everyone else is an incompetent fool with no right to be let loose on the roads.

Once upon a time it was enough to be a good, old-fashioned road-hog. This meant driving around in a state of blissful ignorance of the existence of other motorists. But now there are so many cars, lorries and other hazards on the roads that in order to survive you have to be more than just a road-hog – you have to be a ROADPIG.

A roadpig is truly a pig at the wheel – a driver devoted to making other people's lives a misery.

A roadpig is someone who can drive at a crawl while preventing others from overtaking. He or she is totally without courtesy or consideration, hasn't a clue where the indicator switch is, has never looked in the rear view mirror and will happily drive at speed through a puddle in front of a bus queue. In short, a roadpig is the only type of driver left who can still derive some pleasure from motoring.

This book tells *you* how to be a roadpig. After only a few lessons your friends will not recognize you, and you will be able to turn the ignition key with a whole new sense of purpose.

You too can be a pig at the wheel.

HOW MUCH OF A PIG ARE YOU?

Can you hold your own on today's roads? Are you pig enough to survive among the traffic lights, roundabouts, motorways and other horrors of modern motoring? Dare you go out on the roads until you know the answer?

To find out just how much of a pig you are, simply tick your answers in this Do-it-Yourself test:

1. How many drivers are there on British roads?
    a) 23,600,000
    b) 23,600,000,000,000
    c) Only you

2. You are in a narrow street with enough room for only one vehicle. The car coming towards you has right of way but your car is older and bigger than his, so you pull out into his path. He flashes his lights at you. Does this mean:
    a) 'Come on'
    b) 'Get out of my way you stupid @! X! XX!'
    c) 'Oh, I thought that switch was the windscreen wipers'

3. The outside lane (that's the one on the far right) of a motorway is for:
    a) Overtaking only
    b) Lorries only
    c) Driving in at all times

4. You are approaching a green traffic light and it turns to amber. Does this mean:
   a) Stop
   b) Keep going
   c) Decide when you get there

5. At what position do you have your hands on the steering wheel?
   a) Ten to two
   b) Quarter to three
   c) Nineteen to the dozen

6. You are turning right at a crossroads and a car opposite also wants to turn right (ie across your path). Should you drive:
   a) In front of him
   b) Behind him
   c) Into him

7. How much is your visibility blocked by stickers, dangling skeletons, furry dice etc.?
   a) less than 20 per cent
   b) 20–70 per cent
   c) over 70 per cent

8. What is 'Aquaplaning'?
   a) Taking the Hovercraft to Calais
   b) Sliding on a wet road surface
   c) Something which only happens to other drivers

9. You are in a narrow street. An oncoming 30-ton lorry has pulled out and is thundering towards you. You have the right of way. Do you:
   a) Insist on your legal rights and keep going
   b) Get the hell out of the way
   c) *a)* then *b)*

10. What do you understand by the following road signs?

a) Don't know
b) No left turn
c) No Aborigines

11.

a) Bends for 3 miles
b) Don't know
c) Go to sleep for next 3 miles

12

12.

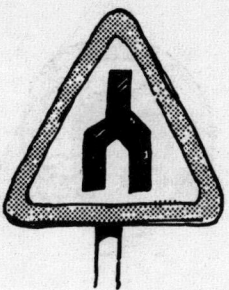

   a) Piano-tuner wanted
   b) Dual carriageway ends
   c) Don't know

13.

   a) Don't know
   b) Bulldozers etc. on road
   c) 60-ton Triffid ambling across road

14.

a) Quayside or river bank
b) Don't know
c) The drive-on ferry hasn't docked yet

15.

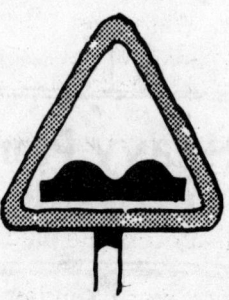

a) Don't know
b) Uneven road
c) You are on the M1

Technical Section

16. What would you do with a Conn Rod?
    a) Obtain money with deception from someone called Roderick
    b) Take it to a garage and say 'Look what's fallen out of the bottom of my car'
    c) Beat husband/wife over head with it when he/she has dented the wing in a car park

17. What is a Rev Counter for?
    a) Taking a census of the number of vicars in a given area
    b) Not sure, but it impresses the girls
    c) Putting down a revolution

18. What is a Wheel Nut?
    a) Someone with a fetish for wheels
    b) Never seen one
    c) Something which you find you should have loosened while the car was still on the ground, when you've just spent half an hour jacking it up before trying to undo it

19. Where would you put a Piston?
    a) Somewhere in the engine
    b) On the carpet round the lavatory
    c) Write an appropriate place to put it: ....

20. You spend every Sunday morning on your back hidden under the car. What do you have with you?
    a) Spanners, sockets and screwdrivers
    b) *The News of the World*
    c) Your neighbour's wife or husband

Now check your score

Question

1.   *a)*   0
      b)   2
      c)   5

2.   *a)*   0
      b)   5
      c)   2

3.   *a)*   0
      b)   2   (lorry drivers score 5)
      c)   5

4.   *a)*   0
      b)   2
      c)   5

5.   *a)*   0
      b)   0
      c)   5

6.   *a)*   2
      b)   0
      c)   5

7.   *a)*   0
      b)   2
      c)   5

8.   *a)*   2
      b)   0
      c)   5

9.   *a)*   0   (There are no marks for attempted suicide)
      b)   2
      c)   5

10. a) 2
    b) 0
    c) 5

11. a) 0
    b) 2
    c) 5

12. a) 5
    b) 0
    c) 2

13. a) 2
    b) 0
    c) 5

14. a) 0
    b) 2
    c) 5

15. a) 2
    b) 0
    c) 5

16. a) 2
    b) 5
    c) 5

17. a) 2
    b) 5
    c) 0

18. a) 2
    b) 2
    c) 5

19. a) 0
    b) 2
    c) 5

20. *a)* 0
  b) 2
  c) 5

How do you rate?

0–30   You're a good, careful driver. Go back
       to the beginning and try again.

30–60   A few flashes of pig-headedness here
       and there, but mostly you're too polite.
       You will need to study the book carefully
       if you want to hold your own on today's
       roads.

60–80   Not bad (ie not good). You clearly have
       streaks of meanness, ignorance and
       arrogance, and have not read your
       Highway Code since you took the driving
       test. A bit more devotion to selfishness
       and incompetence and you could be
       quite a roadpig.

Over 80   Congratulations. You're an utter dis-
       grace. No-one in his right mind would go
       within a million miles of you on the public
       highway. Your car is nothing more than
       a sty on four wheels. Award yourself two
       turnips and a ring through the nose.

KNOW THE ENEMY

The creatures who share the roads with you have not come about by accident. Over the decades evolution has weeded out the weak and encouraged the strong to survive. Your own place in the pecking order is related to your size and engine power. Thus the humblest occupants of the road are:

Hedgehogs
The problem for hedgehogs is that there is some uncertainty about who has the right of way. The other road users tend to travel *along* the road. Rapidly.

Hedgehogs, equally convinced that they have right of way, usually only travel *across* the road. Very slowly. This has unfortunate consequences for the hedgehog.

Cyclists
As far as the average driver is concerned, the only difference between a hedgehog and a cyclist is that a hedgehog travels across his line of sight while a cyclist occupies the blind spot inside his front nearside wing.

There are other differences such as speed of travel, injuries suffered during mating and so forth, but basically hedgehogs and cyclists share bottom place in the pecking order of the road.

In fact, there used to be an even lowlier category of road user, namely a hedgehog on a bicycle, but the mortality rate was so high that the species became extinct. If you *should* happen to see one report it at once . . . to your doctor. He will be very interested.

In an attempt to avoid being spotted, many cyclists travel only at night with no lights.

There are cases, however, of cyclists getting together to fight back. Just as a group of sparrows will gang up on a bullying starling at a bird table, in some cities (Cambridge and Amsterdam, for example) cyclists have learned to flock together and cause vehicular coronaries.

Pedestrians
Pedestrians have the temerity to travel on the highways without the protection of the steel carapace enjoyed by most road users. This is alright where pavements are provided to prevent obliteration. But it is sometimes necessary for them to venture onto the same strip of tarmac as that down which big, lumbering lorries scrape the hedgerows and flatten anything in their paths.

Thus there are two classes of pedestrian: those on a pavement or crossing, and those on the open road. The former enjoy certain immunities. For the survival chances of the latter, however, see under Hedgehogs and Cyclists.

Some pedestrians have, like rats in laboratories, learnt tricks, and have even, occasionally, tamed and dominated the higher orders of road user.

They have, for example, discovered a handful of Pelican crossings where the button actually works. On pressing it, the lights turn red for the marauding traffic which, under the law of the jungle, must sit and watch the prey escape. It may only pounce when the light gives the flashing amber (or 'go get 'em') signal, by which time there may be only one or two old-age pensioners left on the crossing to 'bag'.

Fortunately for the motorist, the button at most Pelican crossings doesn't make a blind bit of difference to the lights and any pedestrian caught unawares is fair game.

Motorbikes

Motorcyclists are the highest order of non-crustacean road users, although they lack the protective steel shell of the crustacean orders, and are far less intelligent (well, what creature with the least vestige of sense would mix with all

21

those cars and lorries on nothing more than a pair of wheels and an engine?)

However, they have evolved to a stage where they have considerable speed and mobility. This means that they are often able to evade their predators by, for example, outsprinting them at traffic lights. Like pedal cyclists, some groups of motorcyclists have learnt to gang up for protection, though this technique is only in an early stage of evolution. So far they have only learnt how to knock the hell out of other motorcyclists.

L or Learner Drivers
L Drivers are the earliest form of crustacean road user. These timid creatures, preyed on by the higher orders, only come out of hiding at certain times, viz:

Rush hours, bank holidays, Saturday mornings (shopping areas), Sunday mornings (coast roads – summer only).

They are also very selective about their terrain, sticking mainly to busy town streets or winding country lanes. Their journeys in the latter case are planned in such a way that there is no traffic coming in the opposite direction while they are negotiating the bends, but streams of oncoming cars appear on the straights when you would like to overtake.

The number of L drivers you are likely to encounter on a particular journey can be calculated from the following equation:

$$L = \frac{H \times T}{A}$$

Where L = the Number of L Drivers on the road at a given time, H = the Hurry you are in, T = the degree of Temper you are in and A = the degree of Absence of any earthly reason why anyone should be out learning to drive at this particular time.

In fact, all crustacean road users started their existence as L drivers, but in their day it was different.

Cars

These are mostly the four-wheeled metal variety, and fall into two species – those more expensive and those cheaper than your own. The former are to be ignored and the latter despised.

There are also some variants, such as cheap cars which look better than yours and expensive ones which – thanks to a streak of inverted snobbery – don't look anything special.

Occasionally, too, you will find a few remaining specimens of nearly extinct lines, such as old crocks and bubble cars. The latter started life when someone had the idea of putting wheels onto redundant Messerschmidt cockpits after the Second World War. However, it turned out to be much safer in a Messerschmidt cockpit at 10,000 feet over Surrey in wartime than to sit in one on the A27 in peacetime, so extinction has nearly been achieved.

If you want to know more about the different categories of car, there are many magazines on the subject. These give details of what they look like, how fast they go, their feeding requirements, longevity etc.

To add to the confusion, tastes keep changing. For example, there was a time when a foreign car was a status symbol. You were really someone, if you drove something with an unpronounceable name. But nowadays, you are regarded as some sort of motoring fifth columnist if you cannot prove that your car was built at Dagenham or Longbridge.

Cars have learnt over the years to survive remarkably successfully. They have developed techniques for evading – and even goading – their predators while nearly exterminating the lower orders. We shall look at some of these techniques in the chapter on Roadcraft.

Builders' Minibuses

There are, in fact, other species of Minibus, but by far the deadliest is the breed which you find during the early rush hour with names like MCQUARRY or JERRY BUILDING CO emblazoned on their sides. Behind the steamed-up windows you can just see the bulky shapes of a small army of men. Although on arrival at the site they may do nothing for the first hour or so, on the road they are in a demoniacal hurry. The throttle has a 'governor' fitted to prevent it from being released from the floorboard, the wing mirrors have long ago been broken off in territorial fights with other road-users, and the driver cannot see out of the back because of an impenetrable mixture of smoke, steam and donkey jackets. He is also unable to see out of the front as the water in the washer bottle was siphoned off to make a pot of tea on the previous site and the wiper blades perished when O'Reilly relieved himself against the scaffolding and the wind was blowing the wrong way.

Builder's Minibuses are mostly ex-getaway vehicles and are capable of impossible speeds.

Faced with a couple of tons of metal at 85 mph which cannot see in any direction and is full of navvies, the lesser inhabitants of the roads are advised to keep a respectful distance.

Coaches and Buses

Coaches are one of nature's little anomalies in that they have not, as one would think, evolved from minibuses. They are more closely related to the giant squid. Like their sea-dwelling cousins they alternate between crawling along at a cumbersome pace (uphill) to sudden jet-propelled bursts of speed (downhill and on motorways).

The relationship to the squid can be most clearly seen when a coach is aroused. Its natural defence is to emit a huge cloud of noxious black fumes and make good its escape while its would-be overtakers cough, splutter and are unable to see where they are going.

Buses are an urban version of the coach. They, too, belch out black smoke and have the added ability of suddenly leaping out from bus stops, causing havoc for other road users. For protection they move round in small convoys and remain in hiding when suspicious of an ambush by waiting pedestrians.

In London, buses have developed a fascinating behaviour pattern. If you look at any time at a bridge over the Thames you will see two buses crossing it in opposite directions. What actually happens is that when the buses reach the ends of the bridge they cross it again the other way in order to give tourists the impression that London Buses abound. Thus the reason that a bus never comes along when you are waiting at a bus stop is that they are all busy going backwards and forwards over the bridges.

Lorries

We now come to the real kings of the road. A lorry's ranking in the order of things can be calculated by the simple method of adding Size + Weight + Speed. Lorries are free from predators as the only creature capable of beating one is an even bigger lorry, and as they all gang up against the rest of the motorized world they are untouchable.

They come in all shapes and sizes, the most impressive being a breed which starts life as a mere head and wheels somewhere on the Continent. By the time it hatches out in Britain it has grown an enormous square shell called a 'container'. At this stage of its life cycle it is unaware that it has grown, for it lumbers through village streets barely wide enough for a horse and cart. Growing all the time it makes its way to the M1 and, joined by thousands of others, heads resolutely northwards to a Juggernauts' graveyard somewhere in Scotland. This legendary spot has never been found.

The largest of the species are known as Abnormal Loads. These giant creatures occasionally venture forth from their hatchery in the depths of the Midlands and labour their way along the busiest road they can find until they eventually run out of energy and die. Their carcasses can sometimes be seen rotting in lay-bys on trunk roads. These magnificent beasts are not in the least bit aggressive, but sadly their extinction is threatened by dwindling supplies of their staple diet.

Caravans

Though smaller than some of their enemies, caravans are capable of dominating most other creatures of the road. A caravan actually belongs to the car species but by evolution it has developed a house-like modification which an otherwise ordinary car can attach to its rear for both attack and defence. Its menacing 'waggle dance' prevents would-be predators from seeing past it and threatens to swipe them off the road if they try to overtake.

Some have grown extra long mirrors out of the side of the car so that the driver can watch with glee as a miles-long column of traffic builds up behind. At holiday times and other crucial periods caravans will congregate on the roads in huge numbers so that if the occasional motorist manages to nip past one caravan he immediately finds himself behind another.

Tractors

Tractors are built like bulls. Most of the time they graze peacefully in the fields and mind their own business. But occasionally a tractor will break through its fence and get onto the road, at which point it becomes extremely dangerous. Its favourite trick is to rumble along at 15 miles an hour and throw huge clods of mud from its wheels at any car which comes up behind and startles it.

A tractor is at its most deadly when it lives on a farm through which a non-motorway dual carriage-

way passes. The beast is quite within its rights to amble out into the left hand lane and then, when the mood takes it, suddenly decide to cross the central reservation to get at the lush grass on the other side.

YOU AND YOUR CAR

Essential Parts

When you take delivery of your car you will find that it has many impedimenta (eg indicators, seat belts, brake lights) but is missing some really vital items. The first thing, then, is to kit the car out with a number of essential extras. These include:

Furry dice, skeletons etc
Nothing makes you more instantly recognizable than having several distracting objects dangling around. Your driver's mirror should be festooned with football boots and other items which are guaranteed to take your eye off the road. Other drivers should be distracted by waving plastic hands or nodding dogs (preferably with luminescent eyes) on the back shelf.

Green visor
Vision should be further restricted by a green transparent strip across the top of the windscreen. If you can still see through this it can be covered with you and your partner's names, eg: Darren & Tracey, Mick & Lorraine, Cyril and Rupert. Not recommended for schizoids, bigamists or car thieves.

Window stickers

You will realize by now that car manufacturers put far too much glass into their machines, so it is important to fill up this agoraphobic space. Spare corners and edges not already occupied by dangling objects and visors can be packed with transfers and stickers, ranging from a memento of a Torbay caravan site to a large slogan saying 'Roadpigs do it in the Middle of the Road', or similar.

Other stickers and badges

Other parts of the car should be decorated in proportion to the pig-headedness of your driving. A few motor sport stickers and a transfer saying 'SUMPSLICK RACING TEAM' will tell other drivers that you have never raced or rallied in your life, while a glittering array of badges on the front bumper can, for a modest outlay and no proven ability, give you a completely groundless feeling of competence and superiority. Finally, you can make people drive too close behind you with a sticker saying 'If you can read this you're too close' in such small letters that the person behind has to mount your rear bumper to satisfy his curiosity and see what it says.

Fog lamps
The 'boy racer' image can be further enhanced by several fog and spot lamps, all with plastic covers which should never be removed. Conversely, the rear fog-light is for switching on at all times, whatever the weather.

Roof rack
Properly loaded, a roof rack can strike terror into the hearts of rival motorists. The trick is to drive round with a precarious pile of chairs, boxes and the occasional pram tied unsafely to the roof, looking as if some or all of it is about to fall into the path of cars behind – or onto the roof of anyone who has the audacity to overtake.

Citizens' band radio
CB radio is a device for occupying one hand and the entire mind instead of concentrating on driving. Inconceivable as it may seem that anyone should want to *look* at the other idiots on the road, let alone *talk* to them, thousands of CB users (appropriately called 'Breakers') happily jabber away to each other as they drive along.

CB radio has two advantages. One is that you can keep broadcasting that there is a terrible traffic jam on the road you are using, thus keeping other drivers away and giving yourself a clear journey.

The other is that when, inevitably, two CB users crash into each other because they are not looking where they are going, they can do all their swearing and shouting over the radio – thus entertaining a much larger audience.

Aerial

Even if you don't have a radio, an aerial is invaluable for being both obnoxious and ostentatious. The favourite type starts as an enormous metal coil – seemingly capable of inducting several thousand volts – and ends in a tip several feet in the air. You may wish to attach a pennant for added distraction, or loop it over the roof and attach the top end to the rear wing, thereby reducing its use as an aerial.

The Parts of the Car – and what to do with them

Having become familiar with the essential items, there are many more fascinating pedals and gadgets worth a passing mention. They include the brakes, accelerator, steering wheel, clutch and gears. A little trial and error may be necessary before you are sure which is which. For example, the two or three pedals on the floor look very similar but after you've pressed the wrong one a few times you'll soon get the hang of it.

Some parts are more important than others. For example, the wheels, whilst not as essential as the dangling skeleton or furry dice, do have a certain desirability. The engine is quite useful, too, as it saves you from having to make two holes in the floor and scurry along with your feet on the ground.

One set of instruments which should be mastered are the many interesting switches and knobs which face you when you sit at the wheel.

Various knobs
In front of you are all sorts of knobs and levers which operate things like the lights, indicators, windscreen washers etc. They all look the same and there is a quaint feeling of serendipity when

operating them. Thus, a loud clicking noise may tell you that when you thought you'd switched on your rear window de-mister half an hour ago it was in fact your hazard warning lights.

Sometimes it is possible to press a button at random and not notice anything different. This leads to a feeling of insecurity as you drive along not quite sure if you have your foglamps on or the bonnet is about to fly open. As a rule of thumb, it is not advisable to adopt a 'let's try this one' approach to unfamiliar switches when travelling at speed.

It is important to learn which stalks and buttons operate the really essential instruments, namely the headlight flasher and horn. Practise hitting them accurately at the first attempt – like the Lone Ranger practising the draw for hours on end – so that in altercations with other drivers you will always honk or flash (or both) first. Nothing is more frustrating than when some swine has just carved you up and you stab at the flasher stalk, only to watch the windscreen wipers sedately grind across the screen. Or you press what you think is the horn and a jet of water splats onto the windscreen.

Headlamps

Note that the headlamps have three settings – side, dip and main beam. One hallmark of a roadpig is pedantry about lighting-up times. Look up the time in your paper each day, then switch on your lights at exactly that time and not a moment before. No matter if it's overcast, gloomy, or as black as your Granny's hat, you can sneer condescendingly at all the other drivers who have got their lights on from sheer ignorance.

The full main beam headlamps have two modes – inexcusable and excusable. The *inexcusable* mode is when someone coming towards you forgets to dip his lights. He should be reminded with much angry flashing to teach him a lesson. The *excusable* version is when, because of all the other important things you have on your mind, you forget to dip your own headlights when someone is coming towards you. Ignore his impatient flashings. He should have more tolerance.

Similarly, it is inexcusable for someone approaching from behind to forget to dip their lights, and much fist-waving is called for. If, however, you happen to forget to lower your lights when coming up behind another car ... well, you're only human.

Seat belts

The subject of seat belts is even better than football for dragging everyone into a heated argument. Half the country believes the law is right to make us wear them and the other half sees them as an affront to individual freedom (as if you have any individual freedom when owning and driving a car).

Like so many things, seat belts aren't half as much fun as they used to be. The original models looked as though they'd been stripped from a Wellington bomber, which was probably often the case. Yards of grey webbing would criss-cross in all directions, culminating in an enormous metal buckle which was sprung like a rat trap to take your fingers off if you weren't careful. They were ideal for young Romeos in the early days of reclining seats. A few quick movements and you could have a damsel in real distress – strapped in and lying down within seconds of telling her you were only pulling in to listen to 'The Archers'.

Today's seat belts are much less exciting. And they also fight back. In the little box which houses the rolled-up webbing there lives a muscular gnome with a perverse sense of humour. You get into the car and grab the seat belt to pull it over your shoulder. The gnome lets it travel a few inches, then digs his heels in and yanks back. The strap stops dead just as you are in full swing and nearly wrenches your arm out of its socket. You stop. The gnome stops. Gently, you tease a few more inches of seat belt out and then there is no reaction. He's asleep. So you heave on the seat belt. No he isn't, he was just fooling you. This time he jerks back and no matter how hard you pull, the damned thing won't budge.

Eventually you get the seat belt on and drive away, but during the journey the little blighter subjects you to a process of slow strangulation mixed with occasional sudden jerks when, for instance, you need to lean forward at a junction to see if anything is coming. The only time he rests is when you actually *want* the seat belt to go back into its hole.

Mirrors
There are two types of mirror – side and rear view. The passenger-side mirror ranks with golf and adultery as a major contributor to the divorce

rate. What happens is that spouse 'A' (often the hapless wife) has to adjust the mirror while spouse 'B' gives instructions from the driving position. The dialogue is one-sided and goes something like this:

'Up a bit and in towards me. Too much. Down a bit. Now you've pushed it out again, all I can see is the +!@! hedge. No, don't tear the thing off, woman. It's not a !o!@ railway coupling. Oh that's great, a perfect view of my left shoulder. Why you can't follow a simple instruction I don't .... here, where are you going? Come back you +!@!+ .....'

And here we leave the happy couple, safe in the knowledge that within two hours of correct adjustment someone will brush up against it and knock it out of alignment again.

Bumpers

These are important items for the roadpig, especially when parking. In America they are known as 'Fenders', which in Britain are things you have on ships. The American term is appropriate there, as their cars are as big as ships anyway.

So much, then, for the various parts of the car. There are many others, but knowledge of them is not necessarily an advantage. It can be the reverse.

Simple Maintenance

Cars, like horses, need to be fed and watered and kept in working condition. Another similarity to their horsey forbears is that the more attention you give them the more they demand, so it's best to stick only to the bare essentials.

Accommodation

A garage is essential. The larger the better, as it will soon fill up with a deep freeze, the lawnmower, wheelbarrow, kids' bicycles, the tumble drier and enough jumble to keep the Womens' Institute in funds for the next 20 years. The car, of course, stays outside on the road.

Feeding

A state of blissful ignorance is the best policy as far as car maintenance is concerned, but one item is unavoidable. The creature does require its regular fill of petrol or it stops, always in the middle of nowhere, when you're in a hurry and it's raining.

Unfortunately the petrol producers have discovered that cars cannot go without their product and they set their prices accordingly. Much fun can be had trying to find a petrol station which is cheaper than the others but it is really quite simple to find the two extremes of the price range by remembering the following infallible rules:

— Petrol is always most expensive at the petrol station at which you've been forced to stop when your tank is almost empty and you don't know how far it is to the next one.

— Petrol is always cheapest at the petrol station immediately *after* the one at which you have just filled up.

Maintenance tips

There are one or two things to learn about running

a car but most of these can be picked up as you go along – if you don't mind learning the hard way.

For example, when you stop the car on a hot day because steam is pouring from the engine, you will soon learn that it is not advisable to undo the radiator cap with your bare hand. Get your passenger to do it instead. Similarly, it doesn't take long to learn that oil should not be poured into the engine through the dipstick hole.

Then there are a few elementary drills to learn, eg: continuous faint knocking noise from rear of car . . . stop, go round to back, open boot, release youngest child, drive on. Or: sudden screeching noise from engine . . . stop, go round to front, open bonnet, release cat, drive on. You'll soon get the hang of it.

As a general rule, though, it's best not to meddle. A car is a very complicated thing and the more 'expert' you become at tinkering with the works the more likely you are to louse it up. Moreover, proper car maintenance requires a degree of competence incompatible with the high standards of incompetence demanded of the average roadpig.

However, if lured by the prestige of being thought to be a DIY wizard, the trick is to buy all the accoutrements – ramps, tools, overalls etc. – and to lie for hours beneath the car . . . *But don't actually touch anything.* That way, whatever may be wrong with the car, you won't make it any worse. Instead, take a good book with you, or simply snooze away a Sunday morning. All that people will see will be your feet sticking out from under the car, so the neighbours will be suitably impressed. Remember occasionally to hit some harmless part of the underbody with a socket handle to give an impressive metallic clinking noise, and before emerging dab some sump oil on your face and hands so you look the part.

The Garage – and how to beat it

Whether you do your own tinkering or not, at the end of the day you will be at the mercy of a garage. Garages have all the equipment and service charts which give them the edge over even the most competent DIY fiend – and a merciless advantage over the average motoring idiot. They know this and charge accordingly. Like farmers, garage owners are always complaining that business is bad and they can't make ends meet. Yet somehow, they always seem to manage to scrape up enough money for the latest Jaguar which is parked beside the new VW in the gravel driveway of a five-bedroom house.

Taking your car to a garage is like going to the doctor. Everything is designed to fill you with a sense of inadequacy and foreboding. When a receptionist eventually condescends to see you he takes out an enormous form and asks a lot of questions which make you feel less than pathetic.:

'Can you *describe* the knocking noise, Sir? Is it coming from the valve tappets or the overhead cam?'

'Is yours the high compression or low compression engine?'

'How many rpm does she idle at on a cold morning?'

And so on. As well as unnerving you and lowering your resistance to the bill, the interrogation tells them how much you actually know about cars so that they can tailor their excuses accordingly. After two weeks of ham-fisted meddling and making the problem worse, they confront you with the prognosis:

'It's a known fault on this particular model, Sir . . .'

'We've done our best guv'nor but if you want my advice it's time you started thinking about a new car. Now I've got a nice little bargain . . .'

'Cars often do that, I'm afraid, but you'll get used to it'.

The fact is that garages have got you by the ball bearings if you try to fight them on their own ground. There's always a valid reason for the fact that twice as much smoke is pouring out of the engine when they've 'mended' it than there was when you brought it in.

The trick is to choose *your* own ground right from the start by appearing to be someone of considerable influence. You could let it drop, for example, that you are the local Euro-MP. This is a safe bet as the title sounds impressive but no-one has a clue who or what their Euro-MP is or does. If, by a million-to-one chance, someone at the garage actually knows the local Euro-MP, then you simply say that you represent the neighbouring constituency, which will have some suitably amorphous name like 'North-West Anglia, Non-Urban'.

Similarly, you could be a JP (having first checked that the garage owner isn't one himself) or a 'Police Federation Adviser'. If all else fails just stick a 'Lord' in front of your name. No-one will know otherwise.

Better still, give the impression that not only are you a VIP, but that you are also immensely knowledgeable about cars, though you prefer not to discuss it. You could, for example, pose as a top-level engineering consultant to an engine manufacturer or specialist car company – one which has no direct connections with your garage, of course.

The VIP trick has a double advantage: the presence of such a prestigious customer throws them off balance and in some cases they may even try to please; and the belief that you have influence and/or mechanical knowledge will discourage them from the more obvious ploys when it comes to bill-and-excuses time.

BASIC ROADCRAFT

The tribulations of owning and maintaining a car are soon compensated for by the pleasures of driving it – provided, of course, that you learn to drive like a true roadpig.

Battle Stance

The first essential is to adopt a suitably pig-like position at the wheel. The most popular is the 'I' was Emerson Fittipaldi's team mate' position:

The hands must grip the wheel, with the whites of the knuckles showing – at exactly a quarter-to-three. The elbows are locked firmly and the arms are in a perfectly straight line from shoulder to wrist. The seat should be back as far as it will go so that the legs cannot fully depress the brake or clutch, but with enough room to push the accelerator straight through the floor pan.

Another popular stance is that of the 'Poison Dwarf' which makes motorists coming up behind unsure if there is, in fact, anyone *at* the wheel. This is ideal for deterring would-be overtakers:

Then there's the 'Natural Pugilist' position – an effective way of convincing other drivers that you are likely to do something horribly unexpected at any moment:

Another good posture for keeping rival motorists

at bay is: 'They drive like this in Kansas where there's nothing else on the road':

A cigarette in the one hand on the driving wheel is an added bonus.

And there are many other, equally fearsome positions. With enough practice it is possible, by holding the bottom of the wheel and using each hand in turn to gesticulate wildly to your passenger, to give the impression that you are not holding the wheel at all. Indeed, you may not be.

If you try out several different postures in secret you will soon find the one which suits you. The hallmarks of a roadpig's driving is that it should:

1. Give you, and only you, the feeling that you are actually in control.

2. Strike fear into the heart of other road-users.

3. Cause your passenger(s) to glance nervously across at frequent intervals to check if you are:
   a) Sane
   b) Awake
   c) Still alive
   d) Any combination of the above

Once satisfied that your position at the wheel is sufficiently intimidating, you are ready to be let loose on the unsuspecting motoring public.

Starting up and Pulling out

First turn the key until the engine fires. Now recover your false teeth and try it again, this time with the engine out of gear.

Next check that the engine is still there by revving furiously several times. By making the engine roar at 5,000 rpm you can impress your neighbours and let the milkman know that it'll be safe to move in soon.

The time has come to pull slowly out into the road. It is important to use the mirror and indicators when starting out, so once you have pulled into the road, look in your mirror and then indicate. This tells the car standing on its nose behind you that you have pulled out.

You are now on your way. Soon you will find that it is much better not to have a destination but simply to take the car out for the hell of it and practise your dreadful driving. This accounts for much of the heavy traffic on today's roads. In recent years the population has only increased by a few per cent, but traffic has doubled because more and more people are driving around aimlessly and fouling up the unfortunate minority who are trying to get from A to B.

What Speed should I Drive at?

You don't have to drive fast to be a successful roadpig. High-speed driving is alright for youngsters who have not yet developed more sophisticated techniques, but it has a major disadvantage – it can kill you, which is not the object of the exercise. If you are dead you can no longer drive like a pig.

Much more important is to learn to *vary* your speed. For example: you are driving along on a sunny Sunday afternoon, harmlessly practising your techniques on a winding country road. You have filled the seats with life-size inflatable dolls, each with a straggly grey wig topped by a black, flowery hat. This gives other motorists the impression that:

a) You are taking a bunch of old dears out for a tootle and scones

b) You do this once a year, the only time your car ever moves outside the garage

c) Because of *a)* and *b)* you are excused luxuries such as indicating, understanding road

signs, knowing where you are or doing anything remotely predictable

At this stage, in one of your rare glimpses in the mirror you spot a car closing fast behind. The occupants are clearly not fellow roadpigs but are actually trying to get somewhere.

Now, the first thing to do is to start making an enormous meal of the bends. At the least hint of a bend, slow down several hundred yards in advance and then brake on the approach as if negotiating the worst hairpin on the St Gotthard pass. *Do not change gear, stay in top.* As you come out of the bend you will see that the other driver, who has been forced to brake and is now breathing down your exhaust pipe, is peering round your offside to see if it's safe to overtake.

At this point, remembering that in your youth it was a toss-up between your job as an accounts clerk or becoming a Formula One racing driver, you should accelerate – still in top gear. After a brief period of harmless juddering you will soon be zooming down the 'straightaway' until the next bend appears and then the slowing-down process is repeated.

The same principle applies on motorways and dual carriageways but the speed changes are more subtle. If, say, you are tootling happily along at 60 mph, your 'target' will be a driver closing from behind who has been going along for some time quite happily at 65. Once he is within number-plate-reading distance, gradually speed up to 64 so that he is now in two minds whether or not to overtake. If it looks as though he is about to accelerate past you, go on up to a speed at which he will give up and return to his original 65. Now slow down imperceptibly and repeat the process.

Variable Speed Driving (VSD) techniques can be used to good effect in most situations – especially on long, straight roads in built-up areas where the car behind can be forced to do unspeakable things to the speed limit when forced in desperation to overtake.

It is also important to remember that the white line down the centre of the road is put there for the guidance of your offside wheels. The more road you can take up, the less people will want to commit themselves to the gutter on the opposite side in order to squeeze past.

Another useful tip is to look dangerously unpredictable (see also: 'Battle Stance') by slowly alternating between hogging the crown of the road and polishing up your passenger doors on the hedgerows.

Very occasionally, you may find yourself behind someone who is going at a satisfactory speed, and you can then stop people overtaking you by pretending all the time to be about to overtake the car in front. This is achieved by pulling out as though to overtake each time you come into a straight, accelerating far too slowly, running out of straight, changing your mind and pulling back into lane just before reaching the next bend. The technique can be kept up for miles, to the increasing frustration of the faster drivers behind you.

The two exceptions to VSD are:

a) When travelling in the outside lane of a motorway or dual carriageway. If you have selected the outside lane as the one in which you wish to travel, then it is important to stick at exactly the legal limit of 70 mph, secure in the knowledge that the character seething at the wheel of the Porsche Turbo behind may not exceed 70 and must therefore be content to stay where he is. You can keep this up for miles, regardless of whether or not there is any traffic on the inside lanes.

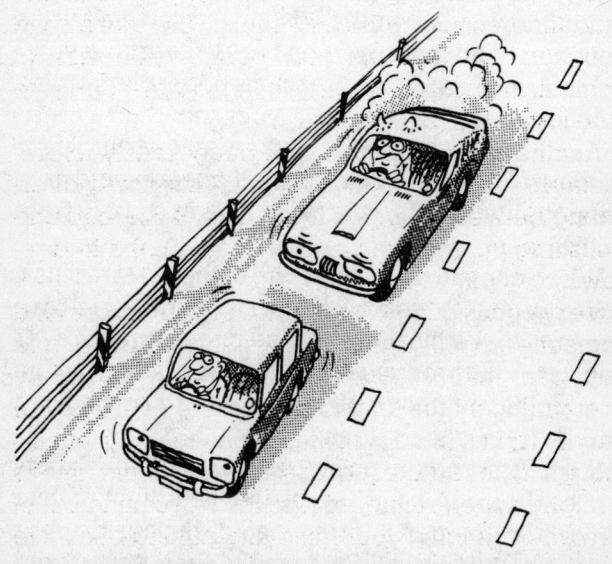

b) When driving in a 30 mph limit in circumstances where 30 is in fact too fast for the conditions (ice, snow, old age pensioners crossing road etc.) Since the signs say 30 then that, of course, is the speed at which you should be travelling.

Overtaking

Clearly, Variable Speed Driving is a vital technique when it comes to overtaking. One of the first things you learn about being a roadpig is that only *you* travel at the right speed. Everyone else on the road travels either too fast or too slowly.

This is an important fact to bear in mind when overtaking. It means that you have a God-given right to overtake every doddering old fool who drives slower than you, and you also have a public duty to stop any maniac who tries to overtake you.

As if you didn't have enough problems with lunatics trying to overtake you, the road is also littered with clowns who think, wrongly, that their tortoise-like crawl is the correct speed – and who have the audacity to try to prevent *you* from getting past.

When coming up behind one of these terrapins it is important to establish early on that you are going to make his life hell if he doesn't move over and let you through. Long before coming within striking range, move out to the centre of the road and start indicating right.

If this first sally is unsuccessful, try a few blasts on the horn and flashes of the headlights while driving with a centimetre or so of his offside rear wing. Should this still fail to make the decrepit old fool move over, you can try lulling him into a false sense of security by dropping back a few yards and resuming a normal position in your lane, with the indicator off. This will make him think that you have submitted and he will a) resume his normal dawdle and b) lose concentration. At this point you change down, accelerate like mad and roar past him when he is looking the other way.

Having successfully overtaken, you can save yourself the effort of reaching for the indicator control. Instead, just keep indicating right in case you should wish to overtake someone else before the end of your journey.

Lastly, there will be occasions when you misjudge your distances while overtaking and there is a car coming the other way. Although theoretically he has the right of way, it is, of course, his duty to be considerate and let you through by slowing down and moving over to the side of the road.

This is not to be confused with the entirely different situation where *you* have the right of way and some demented oaf is overtaking towards you. It is then your duty to flash your lights, hoot frantically, shake your fist and maintain your speed and line. These inconsiderate fools need teaching a lesson.

Indicating

In the good old days there were no such things as indicators. Instead, you simply wound down the window, stuck your arm out, and used your right hand to tell the other road users almost anything you wanted. Thus with a flick of the wrist and a waggle of the fingers you could say: 'I am going to turn left', or 'I have just turned left you stupid !!@*I' or 'Line me up a pint, Florrie, I'll be back when I've found the brake'.

Nowadays, all you have is a choice of small

stalks on the steering column, one of which makes the indicator lights flash. Indicating is regarded as 'sissy' by most roadpigs, but with careful use it can actually enhance the awfulness of your driving.

Say, for example, that you are approaching a traffic light in a built-up area and there are two lanes. The inside lane is straight-ahead-only and you are in the outside one which is marked by arrows showing:

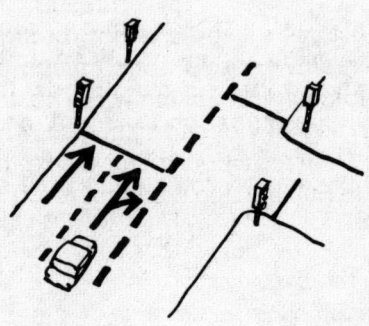

This means that you have the choice of going straight on or right as the mood takes you. If you are going straight ahead you can fool the cars behind you by indicating right. All you are saying – quite correctly – is 'I am in the right-hand lane and am saying so'. However, those following you think 'He is turning right, which will mean that he has to stop at the crossroads and I will get stuck behind him'. They therefore pull in to the long stream of traffic in the left-hand lane and are no longer a possible overtaking menace.

Conversely, if in fact you *intend* to turn right, *Do not indicate* – especially if you are the front car in the lane and the lights have just turned red. By not indicating, you will lure a whole lane of fast traffic into thinking that you are going straight on, so they will line up behind you, revving in anticipation of the lights turning green and the Monaco Grand Prix getting underway. Only when the lights have changed and the oncoming traffic is pouring through do you sit where you are and indicate right. Now you can enjoy another rare look in the rear-view mirror and watch them all cursing and trying to cut back into the inside lane.

This is just one example of how being a successful roadpig can depend not so much on knowing when to indicate as knowing when *not* to.

Another use of non-indicating is when turning left while a car – or better still a stream of them – is waiting to pull out into the main road:

Stage 1

He (thinks): He's slowing down. If he's going to turn left I can get out. But he's not indicating, so maybe he's going straight ahead and I can't pull out.'

You: 'I think I might turn left here'.

Stage 2

He: 'What the hell *is* he doing?'

You: 'I'm turning left, but I don't see why I should tell *you*.'

Stage 3

He: '!@× I'
You: 'Tee hee!'

This tactic is even more effective when you have a stream of ongoing traffic behind you which then stops your victim from getting out for several minutes.

Once you have become an expert at indicating and not indicating, you can use your techniques to devastating effect at roundabouts. If, for example, you indicate right when approaching a roundabout, the drivers behind you do not know if you are going to actually turn right or are merely indicating to get round the first half of the roundabout before going straight ahead. Indicating left causes similar apoplexy for vehicles waiting to pull out onto the roundabout in front of you.

Equally, by not indicating, no-one knows what on earth you are going to do next, yet as long as you are on the roundabout you have right of way.

If you have half-an-hour or so to spare, you can cheerfully go round and round the same round-about, indicating and not indicating in all directions, enjoying the white-faced hysteria of the other drivers.

Turning Techniques

Roads have many things like junctions, turnings, crossroads and cul-de-sacs which greatly increase one's scope for incompetence. Instead of just driving in a straight line, one has to turn the wheel as well. After every journey ask yourself: 'Have I done my bad turn for the day?'

The basic bad turn, and one which every road-pig should master before going on to the more advanced stuff, is the simple left turn. This is also known as the 'Five Course' turn (because you make a great big meal of it).

Stage 1

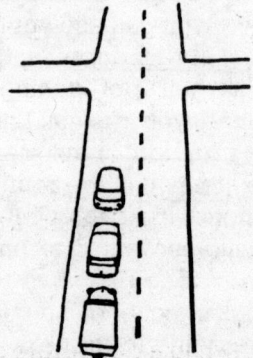

You are driving along and are going to turn left. Only you know this. It is important to let the driver behind you think that you are going straight on.

Stage 2

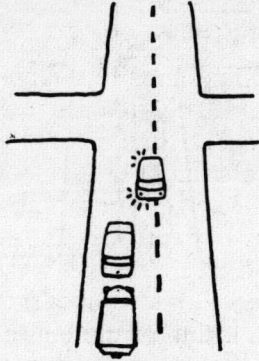

The next stage is most difficult as you have to do three things at once:
— move to the centre of the road
— brake
— indicate left (unless another car is waiting to come out of the side road – in which case see under 'Indicating')

The car behind now knows that you are going to do *something* but doesn't know if you are:
a) Actually going left
b) Turning right but indicating wrongly
c) Not sure yourself

Stage 3
You now slow down to a deliberate crawl and take a wide sweep round to the left as if negotiating a hairpin bend with a 40-ton juggernaut on a one-in-three hill.

But not knowing whether you are going left or

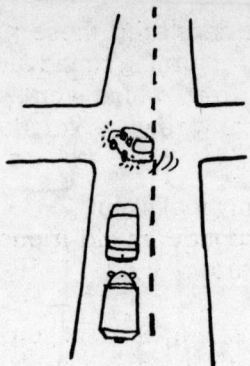

right the following car is uncertain whether to overtake on the inside or the outside, so you can keep him at bay and cause untold frustration.

The converse of this tactic is the right turn, for which the starting point is the nearside kerb.

A similar technique is used at junctions, where you can keep your options open whilst preventing other vehicles from being so audacious as to draw alongside – and possibly even get to their destinations before you get to yours. There are five possible routes:

Once you have mastered these principles you can try your hand at turning round and going back in the direction from which you were coming. There can be many reasons for doing this. For instance:

    a)   You suddenly feel like it
    b)   You have spotted an old friend you haven't seen for years
    c)   You are lost
    d)   You have just realized that you are going the wrong way down a one-way street

Start with an ordinary 3-point turn. As your road-pig technique improves this can become a 4, 5 and 6 point turn. Some top-flight roadpigs can even get into double figures. There is also the 'U' turn, which in your case should be a 'Non-U' turn.

The most fun of all, though, can be had when turning right at a crossroads and an oncoming car also wants to turn right.

The delight of this turn is that you each have the choice of going in front of the oncoming car or behind it. You are really meant to go behind each other but thanks to:

    a)   a clause in the Highway Code which permits you to go in front of each other in certain circumstances, and
    b)   the improbability of either of you knowing the Highway Code,

then two drivers, each faced with two options (and two possible courses by the other driver), can cause almost any combination of disasters. A typical sequence might be:

Stage 1

He (thinks): 'Do I go in front of him or behind him?'
You (think): 'Do I go in front of him or behind him?'

Stage 2

He: 'Is he going to go in front of me or behind me?'
You: 'Is he going to go in front of me or behind me?'

Stage 3

He: 'He's going in front of me, so I'll go in front of him.'

You: 'He's going behind me, so I'll go behind him.'

Stage 4

He: 'Have I paid my insurance premium?'

You: 'Have I paid my insurance premium?'

Traffic Lights

Much of the fun of driving is spoilt by traffic lights. They require you to do unaccustomed things like stopping, anticipating and sometimes even thinking.

The most common form has three lights. To a practised roadpig the colours mean:

Green   Put your foot down and get through before they change

Amber   Put your foot down and get through before they change

Red   You really should have stopped before they changed

Then, whilst waiting at the lights, they mean:

Red   Handbrake off, engage gear, clutch in, start revving

Red and Amber   Go

Green   Get a move on you stupid old goat

To confuse matters, some lights have different signals. There are some, for example, which suddenly flash an amber light on and off. These can be disconcerting as they might mean something nasty like 'pedestrians crossing' or 'drive carefully'.

Then there are lights at roadworks. These are green as you approach them but always turn red before you get there. You then have no idea if the delay is for ten seconds or several hours.

The only certainty is that, as long as you wait for the lights to change, absolutely nothing comes through from the opposite direction. However, the moment you decide that the lights are broken and drive through regardless, at the narrowest point you will meet another vehicle.

Traffic lights at roadworks have a mind of their own. They can spring up from nowhere, often when there is patently no work of any sort going on. When the mood takes them – usually at night when the roads are otherwise deserted – they can sometimes show red in both directions. (At least this is preferable to them showing green in both directions).

Properly used, traffic lights *can* give the roadpig much amusement. For example, when approaching a light which changes from green to amber, he has two choices:

a) Put foot down and belt through at last moment, or

b) stand on brakes

Either action scores points over the driver behind, who is either left cursing at the lights or has to stand on his brakes when he's just bought two dozen eggs and put them on the back shelf.

It is also interesting to look around you at the reactions of other drivers while waiting for the

lights to change – especially when there are two or more lanes. If you appear as nervous as a cat, it can be catching. Grip the wheel and crane forward, peering at the lights as if ready to leap forward the moment they change. All the other drivers will then do likewise in case they are missing something. Then, by revving noisily, you can create the atmosphere of the starting grid at Brands Hatch.

Having got everyone else at fever pitch you can then:

a) Start to creep forward while the lights are still red. This causes all the other cars – and especially lorries – to do likewise, and can sometimes make an unwary victim think that the lights have changed and go roaring off while they are still red.

b) As soon as the lights change you suddenly become a safety-conscious driver and move off very slowly, watching with delight as the vehicles in the other lanes hurtle past in a welter of exhaust fumes and burning rubber, while the drivers behind you fume at not being able to relieve their frustrations. A similar effect can be achieved by stalling at the critical moment.

Traffic Jams

The trouble with having lots of roadpigs wandering around aimlessly is that they often all end up in the same place. This means having to sit for ages waiting to get through a bottleneck simply because of a bunch of idiots who have no right to be there.

Some classes of vehicle have an advantage in traffic jams, notably lorries and motorbikes.

Lorries love hot days when everyone sitting in the jam has the windows open and the fan on. Undoubtedly, there is a little man at every lorry depot whose job it is to see that the maximum amount of filthy black diesel smoke pours out of the exhaust, which is usually sited as near as possible to the air intakes of surrounding cars. Other road users in a traffic jam on a hot day thus have a choice of either choking to death or shutting the windows and turning the fan off, thereby roasting to death.

A motorcyclist can infuriate other motorists by picking his way through impossible-looking gaps and getting ahead of all the cars who have just gone to great lengths to overtake him.

For the average motorist a traffic jam is exasperating. Every minute spent stationary feels like an hour of motoring time. The engine over-heats, you overheat, your passenger reminds you ad nauseam that he or she said to go the back way, and any kids who have not already been car-sick now want to go to the toilet. It is even worse when there is more than one lane of traffic as you are bound to be in the wrong one. The law of traffic jams is that the fastest-moving lane is always the one in which you are not.

But for the conscientious roadpig a traffic jam can be a source of endless amusement. Instead of sitting there helplessly you can think of some absorbing games to play which are guaranteed to drive the other occupants of the jam into a state of advanced hysteria.

For instance, there's 'Honkers'. Choosing a moment when it is obvious that no-one can possibly move an inch in any direction, give a sudden blast on the horn. All the other drivers will glare accusingly at each other, trying to locate the impatient moron who can't see that the traffic is stuck, so remember to look round accusingly yourself. That way no-one will be sure who is actually doing the honking.

Once everyone has settled down again, give another honk on the horn. Keep the blasts short so that no-one can identify the source. At this stage you can leap out of the car and glare up and down the road, showing righteous indignation at the mystery honker.

Soon, another driver in the queue, convinced that the hold-up is all the fault of some indecisive cretin at the front, and dying for an excuse to vent his feelings, will follow suit and blast his horn. Eventually, you can get the entire traffic jam blasting away furiously and shaking their fists at each other.

Another delightful game is 'Creepers'. If you watch people's reactions in a traffic jam you will see that each time the car in front moves forward, the next car automatically moves up to fill the gap – no matter how small.

'Creepers' is played by staying put when the traffic in front edges forward, allowing a decent gap of, say, 10–20 yards to develop. The next step is to move forward by an insignificant amount of one or two yards, then stop and watch in the mirror. The driver behind will faithfully get into gear, handbrake off, rev up and move forward to fill the gap. Whereupon the driver behind does likewise, and so on back down the line. As soon as the last car in the queue has moved forward you then move on another two yards and watch them go through it all again.

The one thing *not* to do in a traffic jam is to be tempted into following the car which turns off into a side road with a look about him which says, 'I know the way round this lot'. If you do so, all will be well at first. He will nip speedily around the back roads with you in close pursuit. You experience a feeling of smugness as this new-found friend pilots you through the depths of the suburban jungle. He will then turn into his own drive at 23, Aspidistra Avenue – and you will be a roadpig in a poke.

Parking

Parking your car is the true test of pig-headed driving. No other aspect of driving embraces so many virtues at once – stupidity, belligerence, thoughtlessness, incompetence, foul language – everything you've ever dreamed of.

The problem with parking is:

a) It demands a degree of skill, which is anathema to the dedicated roadpig

b) There are less parking spaces than people who want to park

c) Parking places are always sited as far as possible from your destination

All the most desirable spots contain traps such as parking meters, yellow lines and 'Residents only' signs. Some car parks – notably multi-storey ones – lure you in by offering no obstructions but then won't let you escape until you pay at the exit. Others have a ticket machine miles away from your parking space, into which you must put 5p pieces if you only have 10p pieces on you, and vice versa.

And wherever you go, lurking in the background, will be a traffic warden. He or she will not be in evidence when you park, but will be skulking round the corner waiting for your time to expire. They are trained to lull you into a false sense of security by ignoring obvious offenders like the Rolls Royce standing all day on a double yellow line in the town centre, so that you think it's safe to stop outside the Chinese take-away for 30 seconds on a faded single yellow line. Then they pounce.

There are many ways of combating traffic wardens but, like the common cold, no truly effective defence has been found. Some roadpigs keep a notice permanently on the windscreen saying 'Press', or 'Doctor on Call', or 'Broken Down'. Unfortunately, traffic wardens have long experience of such ruses, which is why journalists, doctors and broken-down motorists pay out more in parking fines than anyone else. One of the more subtle ploys is to leave a copy of the *Police Gazette* ostentatiously on the back seat or to fit a 'CD' immunity plate to the car, but even these are no guarantee against the wiles of the traffic warden.

The first rule of atrocious parking is to take up as much room as possible. Points are scored for the number of spaces you can occupy with one car. Many parking areas provide helpful white lines to enable you to do this. Some are single rows thus:

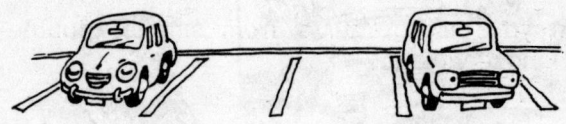

in which the object is to try to get as centrally over a white line as possible, thus:

Advanced roadpigs, especially those with long cars, may wish to try the 'three in a bed' technique:

The next stage up is 'noughts and crosses' which is played on multiple spaces:

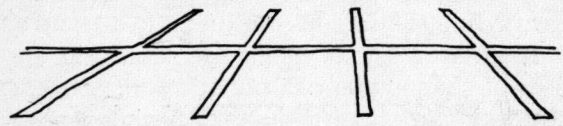

Here you can graduate from simple, double-blocking techniques . . .

to the highly advanced 'four leaf clover' . . .

. . . while with a large enough car you could even extend the 'three in a bed' technique to take up six spaces and score maximum points.

Where there are no white lines to guide you, greater skill and judgement are required. For example, you may find a kerbside situation where there is a gap for two cars:

Here the obvious technique is to park as centrally as possible:

However, if the car in front is parked too close to the next car it can be more fun to park up against his bumper so that he can't get out – particularly if you are going to be away from your car for a long time:

Where there is only room for one car you must pounce quickly as there may already be someone trying – for reasons beyond comprehension – to go in backwards, thus:

By moving fast enough you can both frustrate the other driver and leave your car blocking half the road:

Or, by way of a change, you can sacrifice the road-blocking in favour of catching unwary pedestrians by leaving a wheel (or, for maximum points, half a tyre's width) up on the kerb.

Other point-scoring parking spots include:

a) across a driveway
b) on the crown of a bend
c) on the crown of a hill
d) opposite another parked car

As a fascinating diversion on a wet Saturday morning or during the evening rush hour, you can play 'Fumbles'. This is played in five easy stages:

1. Drive into a multi-storey car park and pull a ticket from the machine, which lifts the barrier to let you in.
2. Park (see techniques above).
3. Forget where you put the ticket.
4. Spend ages fumbling for the ticket at the exit barrier while an angry queue builds up behind you.
5. Find your ticket, then repeat the fumbling action for correct change.

Signs

In the good old days road signs used to say what they meant. Thus, if you were required to stop, a sign would simply say 'Stop'. Or you could tell if you had just driven the wrong way down a one-way street by looking back and seeing a sign which said 'One Way Street'. Steep hills and other hazards were similarly marked.

Then one day some bureaucrat discovered that road signs in plain English were dangerous for *a)* foreigners and *b)* illiterates, who together represented about two per cent of the motoring population. So all the road signs were put into pictures, which the foreigners and illiterates could understand but the remaining 98 per cent couldn't make head nor tail of.

Thus, a good old 'Danger, Steep Hill' sign might now say:

which means that by the time you've worked out what the sign means – and what the hell kind of a gradient 20 per cent is – you have shot over the edge and are travelling down the cliff face at a gradient of 100 per cent.

Or you might pass some alarming picture such as:

which could mean anything from 'You are about to be struck by Lightning' or 'Beware low flying Superman'.

Some are horrifyingly confusing. For example:

These are guaranteed to throw any respectable roadpig into an instant panic, not knowing if he should be going in both directions at once, no direction at all, or has just driven into the launderette.

Even worse are the signs painted on the road. These suddenly spring up at you when you are not concentrating. One of the most prolific is the 'box junction':

on which you suddenly find you are sitting when you have followed a queue of vehicles through a traffic light, they have stopped suddenly, the lights have changed against you and you can go neither forward nor back. The hatched yellow lines tell you that you shouldn't be there at all, which is little consolation.

Another favourite is the arrow which, with no prior warning, informs you that you are in the wrong lane. This occurs when you are happily overtaking in the outside of two or more lanes and come to a red traffic light. At this point a large right-turn-only appears on the road beneath you:

By the time you discover the arrow, it is impossible to get back into the inside lane and the traffic behind is honking at you to get a move on and turn right.

Some arrows even lure you into thinking that your lane does, in fact, go straight ahead. The first arrows say:

followed by:

then, once you are stuck in the outside lane with no hope of return to the inside, the trap is sprung:

Nor is there any point seeking refuge in the inside lane. This is equally prone to left-only arrows which can send you looping off towards Slough when you are trying to get to Potter's Bar.

Motorway signs provide yet another kind of horror. These add to your normal worries by consisting of lots of little lights, some of which are flashing.

Imagine your dismay when you are happily poodling down the M4, blissfully unaware of anything beyond the blare of the radio and the skeleton dangling peacefully from the driver's mirror, when one of these looms up:

Suddenly the tranquillity of the journey is shattered. This flashing monstrosity is telling you that something nasty is about to happen but you don't know what. It's the same feeling as when one of the dashboard warning lights comes on . . . you don't have a clue what it means but you know that it's bad news.

Then, just as things seem to be settling down again, one of these leaps out at you:

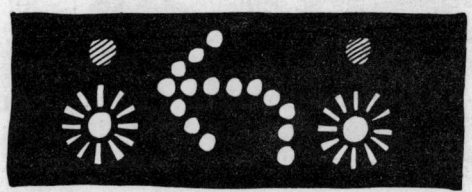

By now your nerves are in shreds and the journey ruined. You still don't know what the flashing signs are all about but would not be surprised to encounter a squadron of flying saucers over the next rise.

All in all, road signs are guaranteed to spoil the fun of driving. It can sometimes be tempting to look them up in the Highway Code to see what they mean, but it's like having your palm read. You want to know what's in store for you but are afraid to ask in case it's something horrible.

Back Seat Drivers

(Note for women readers: for 'wife' please read 'husband' and for 'she' and 'her' read 'he' and 'him'.)

'Back Seat Driver' is a misnomer as it refers to someone who directs operations from the front passenger seat. The best form of defence against a Back Seat Driver is to go on the offensive. Before you even start the journey, take her mind off your own incompetence by getting her worried about all the other dreadful drivers on the road. You could start with:

'I should do your seat belt up securely if I were you. I drive safely enough but you never know when some maniac's going to drive into you'.

And try a product diversion, such as:

'Whoever designed this car obviously never had to sit in it. I've never known such an uncomfortable seat'.

Then devote the entire journey to criticizing everybody else's mad driving:

'I knew that fool was going to pull out in front of me'.

'Good God, she actually looked in her mirror'.

'That old goat shouldn't be allowed out in a bath chair, let alone a car'.

'Sorry about that but I had some idiot breathing up my exhaust pipe'.

And so on. This approach channels her fears and frustrations in the direction of other road users . . . and also stops her getting a word in edgeways.

If the back seat driving persists, as a last resort get *her* to do the driving.

DRIVING ABROAD

If by now you fancy yourself as a roadpig you may be ready to try your hand at driving overseas. However abysmal you think the standard of driving is in Britain, you ain't seen nothing 'til you've diced with death on the *autobahns* of Germany or done battle in the streets of Rio de Janeiro.

For one thing, all foreigners drive on the wrong side of the road, ie on the right. In many Southern Hemisphere countries they appear to drive on the left, but this is really the right, only upside-down. For example, in places like Japan and New Zealand they drive 'on the left' in the same way as the water goes the wrong way down the plug-hole.

In countries which the Equator crosses (eg in Africa and South America) drivers try to keep to the same side of the road, as you can't really have half the country driving on the left and half on the right! In fact, in Africa and South Africa it doesn't really make much difference which side of the road you drive on anyway.

Below are just a few of the situations you may encounter in foreign parts:

Germany

For devotees of pig-headed driving, Germany is the Mecca. The first thing you notice is the dead-straight *autobahns* (motorways). They are built this way so that the Germans can hurtle down them with one hand on the horn and one on the head-lamp flasher – there being no need to steer.

German drivers are highly knowledgeable about the law and the highway code, and kill off vast numbers of other road users in the name of 'correctness'. For example, if you are a German driving in a built-up area at 50 kilometres per hour (whatever the conditions it must be exactly 50) and you are on the correct side of the road, then no matter what crosses your path – be it a pensioners' outing or the Four Horsemen of the Apocalypse – you are in the right. So you must keep going.

There is no speed limit on the *autobahns*, which means that you cannot smugly occupy the outside lane at a constant 70 mph as drivers do in this country. Instead, every occupant of the outside lane is a 'Gott-vorsaken Dummkopf' getting in the way of the car behind. Thus they pursue each other like fish being eaten by bigger fish, which are being eaten by bigger fish, which are being eaten ... The flashing lights and horns are reminiscent of a disco on Saturday night.

For further information on driving in Germany, consult 'Strassenfuehrer' (ie Fuehrer of the Roads), by Blindasbatt and Halfpisst.

Italy

No-one has got around to telling the Italians that there are any stages between having the feet off the brake and accelerator pedals and having them flat on the floor. So everyone drives along in a series of dragster-like accelerations and tyre-screeching emergency stops.

The principle when changing lanes, approaching junctions etc is that you keep going until the other driver loses his nerve and gives way – which is alright if it works. Unfortunately, much of the time neither driver loses his nerve, which is why Italian cars are made small, cheap and tinny. The insurance companies never pay out, so you don't want to spend too much on replacing your car every few weeks.

Driving is particularly lunatic on the *autostradas* (motorways), which have replaced the old chariot tracks in the amphitheatres as entertainment. Such is the pleasure derived from playing high-speed dodgems on these *autostradas* that the Italians actually pay large sums to go on them.

France

The French drive much like the Italians, but without the same care and restraint.

Belgium

The standard of driving in Belgium has to be seen

(preferably from a considerable distance) to be believed. Actually, there are sound demographic reasons for the fact that the whole country is one big pool table of collisions and ricochets.

You see, no-one actually goes *to* Belgium. They only go *through* it. The roads are therefore full of French drivers going to Germany and the Netherlands, and German and Dutch drivers going to France – in other words, three of the worst driving nations are all on their way to play havoc on each other's roads. They meet, head-on, in Belgium.

The mayhem is exacerbated by the fact that the Belgians, have adopted all the worst driving habits of their closest neighbours – the French, Dutch and Germans.

North America

As a general rule the further you go from Britain the more atrocious the standard of driving; but the

United States is different. The high murder rate, not to mention the incidence of fires, earthquakes and other natural disasters, enables the Americans to relieve their frustrations in a number of other ways before taking to the roads.

However, if the driving still has a certain colonial charm, at least the motoring terminology is redolent of gangsters and violence. For example, our genteel-sounding 'bonnet' becomes a sinister 'hood' and the simple 'boot' is a 'trunk', ie a thing you keep bodies in!

South America

For some really hairy motoring you need to travel south a few thousand miles. This is the part of the world where sugar cane is distilled into alcohol

and now fuels 40 per cent of the cars . . . and 80 per cent of the drivers.

Middle East

There are fewer cars in the middle East than elsewhere, but the inhabitants make up for this by taking up the entire road. They are assisted in this by having particularly large cars.

It has long been thought that desert people used to travel by camel before the advent of the car, but in fact it was the other way round. The roads in the Middle East are so dangerous that anyone with a grain of sense buys a camel and gets as far away from the public highways as possible – hence the presence of people on camels in the middle of the desert.

Japan

Japan is ideal for the gregarious type of roadpig who likes to be surrounded by zillions of other motorists.

The Japanese have a problem. Having created a motor industry which churns out increasingly large numbers of cars, they now don't know how to stop it. As a result millions of new cars pour onto the roads every year. This means that they are putting more and more robots into the factories to make the cars, thereby releasing the people to drive them.

Once the entire population of 100-odd million is doing nothing else but drive round all day, the Japanese will programme the robots to make each car with its own driver-robot so that an infinite number of cars can be driven onto the roads. If you think the traffic in Tokyo is bad now, you should see it in another ten years.

Australia and New Zealand

In contrast, Australia and New Zealand are for the roadpig who wants the entire road to himself. There are large areas of these two countries where the roads have been built but cars haven't caught up with them. This spoils some of the pleasure for a roadpig, as half the fun is to have other motorists around to harass, but at the same time it's nice to get away from it all occasionally.

So now that you've finished *A Pig at the Wheel* and are a fully qualified roadpig, why not go and find yourself a nice quiet corner of the Great Sandy Desert to drive around in for a while.

Maybe longer.